YEATS' IRELAND

YEATS'
IRELAND

JOHN GREGORY

CAXTON EDITIONS

FIRST PUBLISHED IN GREAT BRITAIN IN 2000 BY CAXTON EDITIONS
A member of the Caxton Publishing Group
20 Bloomsbury Street, London, WC1B 3QA

ISBN 1 84067 1343

A copy of the CIP data is available from the
British Library upon request.

Designed and produced for Caxton Editions
by Keith Pointing Design Consultancy.

Reprographics by GA Graphics
Printed and Bound in Singapore by Star Standard Industries

Front Cover illustration courtesy of
the National Gallery of Ireland,
'The Heart of Old Dublin, St Patrick's - Swift's Cathedral',
painted in 1887 by Walter Osborne (1859-1903)

Acknowledgments
Mr and Mrs Feeney, Lissadell View, County Sligo,
Eamon Martin, Dublin, Irene O'Reilly, London.

CONTENTS

INTRODUCTION

I<small>T MATTERS NOT</small> that William Butler Yeats was born in Dublin,

that he passed much of his childhood in London, or that in later life

he divided most of his time between these two capital cities when he

was not travelling further afield, to America on lecture tours or to

France for a vacation. Artists tend to be restless souls, after all, and

W B's endless wanderings began when he was still a child and his

father, the portrait painter John Butler Yeats, upped sticks and

L<small>EFT</small>: *The rock of Cashel.*

moved to London, where the family moved from one house to the next on a regular basis. Perhaps it was so many changes of address during childhood that habituated the poet and playwright of later years to a life of outward peregrination.

And yet, if one turns to his internal life, to what he felt were his roots, to the life-force that fed his poetic imagination, then he had only one true home. For it is to Ireland, and particularly to its wild, westernmost parts, that Yeats is constantly returning in spirit – if not always in person. His very first memories of childhood, fragmentary and jumbled-up though they be, are of "sitting upon somebody's knee, looking out of an Irish window at a wall covered with cracked and falling plaster, but what wall I do not remember, and being told that some relation once lived there."

And it seems from that moment on, Yeats always thought of Ireland as both his homeland and his source of inspiration.

Through all those childhood years in London – which he plainly detested – the one joyful prospect appears to have been the impending holidays. When he was sent back to his relations in County Sligo. His excitement at reaching the Liverpool docks, from whence he took ship for Ireland, is palpable. But when the holidays were over, he had to return to London and his education at the Godolphin School in Hammersmith, where he was frequently "called names for being Irish" and felt very much the outsider. So much so that he sought means of retaliation.

"There was a boy with a big stride", he recalls: "much feared by little boys, and finding him alone in the playing-field, I went up to him and said, 'Rise upon Sugaun and sink upon Gad'. 'What does that mean?' he said. 'Rise upon hay-leg and sink upon straw', I answered, and told him that in Ireland the sergeant tried straw and hay to the ankles of a stupid recruit to show him the difference between his legs. My ears were boxed, and when I complained to my friends, they said that I had brought it upon myself; and that I deserved all I got. I probably dared myself to other feats of a like sort, for I did not think English people intelligent or well-behaved unless they were artists."

The sadness of an exile's existence, this longing for distant Sligo, may have been instinctive, though, as the poet later recognised, both were actively encouraged by his mother, Susan Pollexfen:

"She would spend hours listening to stories or telling stories of the pilots and fishing-people of Rosses Point, or of her own Sligo girlhood, and it was always assumed between her and us that Sligo was more beautiful than other places".

RIGHT: *Galway*

Yeats stood in great awe of his grandfather, the ship-owner and former sea-captain William Pollexfen, who "had won the freedom of some Spanish city, for saving life perhaps, but was so silent that his wife never knew it till he was near eighty, and then from the chance visit of an old sailor".

For all his romantic adulation of his maternal grandfather, Yeats was very much aware that both sides of his family were solidly Protestant and middle-class. He liked to draw attention to the military and other exploits of his ancestors on the Yeats side, who had been in Ireland more than 200 years. And yet he did not consider himself any less of an Irishman for his Protestant background. Indeed, from the earliest years when he listened to mother telling of the pilots and fishing-people, and how both she and the servants had heard the banshee crying the night before his younger brother Robert died, he was instinctively sympathetic to the mysteries embedded in Ireland's rich folk-lore, forever on the look-out for any wise-man or – woman with their tales of the faerie-people, for any supernatural or unexplained occurrence, that might add to this internal treasure.

From this deeply-rooted belief in the spirit world, in things hidden and inexplicable by reason alone, sprang some of the most powerful themes and images of his later poems. Certainly, his early exposure in Sligo to tales of banshees wailing and faeries batting upon the waters encouraged him later on in life to explore the whole realm of Celtic mythology, and to draw inspiration from it in his work as a dramatist as well as his poetry. It was also the beginning of a long spiritual journey that would carry him much further afield, to the spiritualism of Madame Blavatsky and an abiding fascination with séances, the dream-world and automatic writing, to an informed interest in Hinduism, Buddhism, and other esoteric teachings of the East; and, finally, to an austere if ill-defined spirituality that finds its true voice only in his later poems.

Dublin was the setting for much of Yeats life journey; and it is there we follow him next. For his painterly father returned to Ireland in 1880, settling first just outside Dublin at Howth and subsequently in the southern suburb of Rathgar. It was in this "fair city" that the future poet spent his adolescence and wrote the first of his poems to be published. And it was here that Yeats entered the frenetic world of the theatre, seeking to build up a distinctly Irish tradition both in the writing of plays and in their performance. It was among Dubliners that he sought his audience; and with some of them he fought his greatest battles. The legacy of all these conflicts and passions is the Abbey Theatre, still standing there in the heart of Dublin.

By now Yeats was recognised as a major poet and a successful play-wright. But if Dublin was the stage on which much of the external drama was played out, his interior life grew more and more apart. He sought a place to withdraw from the world; and this he found first at Coole Park in County Galway, and then in the medieval tower not far away, Thoor Ballylee, in which he made his home. To this hidden corner of Galway we must follow him if we are to find the quiet places that breathe life into some of his greatest poetry.

But to discover the origins of Yeats' poetic genius, we must go back with him to Sligo – to its myth-laden mountains, its enchanted forests and reverie-inducing loughs. For it was Sligo's sly magic that slipped into his consciousness before all else; and it was there, beneath Ben Bulben, that he would be laid to rest after his consciousness had departed.

I

SLIGO

I FIRST WENT down to Sligo Bay during my school holidays. The outing was suggested by a friend of Anglo-Irish ancestry who had first introduced me to the poetry of W.B. Yeats. We would take a bus down the coast where we were camping in Donegal, our well-thumbed copies of the *Collected Poems* stuffed into duffel-coat pockets, and see where the Great Man was buried "under bare Ben Bulben's head."

LEFT: *Parkes Castle, Lough Gill on the Leitrim/Sligo border.*

It was a schoolboys' impromptu attempt at a literary pilgrimage; and, as is often the case with such outbursts of enthusiasm, it was not an unmitigated success. Through slanting rain we laboured up Ben Bulben's flank, and when we finally reached the top had little recompense; for now the mountain's flattened crown was wreathed in cloud, thus robbing us of one of Ireland's finest views. To cap it all, my ankle went over during the descent, so it was a bedraggled and half-lame contingent that eventually crawled into the churchyard at Drumcliff.

We found the slab of local limestone, and read the final verses incised upon it. With heads uncovered and the rain still slanting down, we stood in silence, each occupied with private thoughts. Then, since the weather showed no sign of letting up, we hopped on a bus into Sligo Town, where we had tea and cake in the

RIGHT: *St Columba's Parish Church, Drumcliff, Church of Ireland.*

wonderfully old-fashioned Café Cairo in Wine Street surrounded
by some elderly and very genteel ladies. There was much about the
town still – the old shop fronts and pubs and decayed warehouses
down by the quays – that Yeats might have recognised. For Sligo
then was trapped within a time-warp – the kind induced by gradual
impoverishment, where nothing changes because the money is too
tight even to contemplate it. Outside in the rain, beggars stood
hopefully on street corners. There were tinkers encamped just
beyond the town limits. Back then, Ireland had not yet joined the
European Community and times were hard, especially in a place so
far removed from Dublin as Sligo. With the port, the mills, the
brewery all gone, the town's fortunes had declined since Yeats' day.

LEFT: *Stone walls and Church ruins,*
near Innisfree, Lough Gill.

Happily, all that is history. For Sligo Town has undergone a renaissance – not without a little help, it may be said. from her "favourite son" W. B Yeats. For over forty years now, the Yeats Summer School has drawn students and scholars of Anglo-Irish literature from far afield, and most evenings productions of W B.'s plays are staged at the Factory Theatre or the Hawk's Well. The whole town has much more youthful, optimistic air about it, having attracted a resident artistic community. On a Friday or Saturday night the pubs are crammed with young people, and no matter whether you end up in Hargadon's, with its labyrinth of secretive snugs and topsy-turvy shelves laden with 19th century bottles, or in Shoot the Crows – thus named because a previous landlord lost patience with the birds nesting on his chimney and fired at them right up the flue – the porter flows as fast as the Garavogue River empties into Sligo Bay.

RIGHT: *Bronze sculpture of Yeats.*

Down by the river there is now a Yeats Building, with an audio—
visual show dedicated to the poet; while just across Hyde Bridge,
in Stephen Street, the Sligo Museum maintains a special section on
W.B., adorned with paintings by his brother, the artist Jack Yeats,
and portraits of the Gore-Booth sisters and other acquaintances.
Between these two stands a statue of the poet, cast in bronze.
I wondered what he would have thought of so much activity done
in his name, but the statue on its plinth offered no clues.
Yeats did not write that much of Sligo Town itself His earliest
memories are of Merville, his grandparents' house; and grandfather William Pollexten did indeed maintain a large establishment.
W.B's sister, Lily, recalls it as "a solid house, big rooms – about
some fourteen bedrooms, stone kitchen offices and a glorious
laundry smelling of soap full of white steam and a clean coke fire
with rows of irons heating at it. Our grandmother's store-room like
a village shop – a place with windows and fireplace shelves and

LEFT: *View of Ben Bulben from Rosses Point.*

a village shop – a place with windows and fireplace shelves and drawers and a delicious smell of coffee – the house was of blue grey limestone – the local stone – 60 acres of land round it – a very fine view of Ben Bulben from the front of the house"

Sadly, the house is there no more. But what Merville, and Sligo Town as a whole, gave to the youthful Yeats was a sense of belonging. Partly it had to do with security, the family's well-established status in Sligo society. As an aunt once cruelly told him: "You are going to London. Here you are somebody. There you will be nobody at all." But there was more to it than that. Many years later he mused about how "those, who like the present writer, have spent their childhood in some small western seaboard town and who remember how it was for years the centre of their world, and how its enclosing mountains and its quiet rivers became a protection of their life forever." Yet even here, he moves swiftly on from town to countryside. For it was out there, amidst Sligo's softly wooded

RIGHT: *Sheep farmer, with dogs in a country lane, Sligo.*

valleys, that he found both inspiration and subject matter for some of his finest poems.

His wanderings began at an early age. All around Sligo there were many uncles and aunts to visit. Sometimes these forays had the added attraction of being forbidden.

"When I must have been still a very little boy, seven or eight years old perhaps, an uncle called me out of bed one night, to ride the five or six miles to Rosses Point to borrow a rail-way pass from a cousin. My grandfather had one, but thought it dishonest to let another use it, but the cousin was not so particular. I was let out through a gate that opened upon a little lane beside the garden away from earshot of the house, and rode delighted through the moonlight, and awoke my cousin in the small hours by tapping on his window with a whip. I was home again by two or three in the morning and found the coachman waiting in the little lane. My grandfather would not have thought such an

adventure possible, for every night at eight he believed that
the stable-yard was locked, and he knew that he was
brought the key."

And there were many other times he would go out to Rosses Point,
with its fishermen's cottages and boats drawn up along the strand, to
see his cousin George Middleton and go on boating trips.

Already Yeats had begun his long voyage into invisible worlds. As he
recalled:

"it was through the Middletons perhaps that I got my
interest in country stories, and certainly the first faery-
stories that I heard were in the cottages about their houses."

And Rosses Point became for him a place "of unearthly resort
... choke-full of ghosts. By bog, road, rath, hillside, sea-border, they
gather in all shapes, headless women, men in armour, shadow hares,

fire-tongued hounds, whistling seals and so on." While from out in Sligo Bay came the "slow low note" of the bell on a storm-tossed buoy.

As he grew older, Yeats "no longer cared for little shut-in places ... and began to climb the mountains, sometimes with the stable-boy for companion, and to look up their stories in the county history." He even tried his hand at fox-hunting, mounted on his red pony. But W.B. readily confessed to be being a timorous horseman, only too happy to abandon the chase and lay down among the ferns looking up at the sky. His delicate sensibility also came out when he rode over to Castle Dargan:

> "where lived a brawling squireen, married to one of my Middleton cousins... It was, I daresay, the last household

RIGHT: *The waterfall at Glencar.*

where I could have found the reckless Ireland of a hundred years ago in final degradation. But I liked the place for the romance of its two ruined castles facing one another across a little lake, Castle Dargan and Castle Fury."

It is still a romantic spot on a summer's evening. the almost bare castle mounds rising above the still waters where Yeats:

"fished for pike ... and shot at birds with a muzzle-loading pistol until somebody shot a rabbit. From that on" he concluded, "I would kill nothing but dumb fish."

Yeats' expeditions became gradually more ambitious and took on more of a literary or spiritual character. Thus, he informed an indulgent uncle:

"I was going to walk round Lough Gill and sleep in a wood. I did not tell him all my object, for I was nursing a

RIGHT: *Fishing boat at Mullaghmore Head.*

new ambition... I planned to live some day in a cottage

on a little island called Innisfree, and Innisfree was

opposite Slish Wood where I meant to sleep.

I thought that having conquered bodily desire and

the inclination of my mind towards women and love, I

should live, as Thoreau lived, seeking wisdom...

I set out from Sligo about six in the evening, walking

slowly, for it was an evening of great beauty; but though

I was well into Slish Wood by bedtime, I could not sleep,

not from the discomfort of the dry rock I had chosen

for my bed, but from my fear of the wood-ranger. I came

home next day unimaginably tired and sleepy, having

walked some thirty miles partly over rough and boggy

ground. For months afterwards, if I alluded to my walk,

my uncle's general servant (not Mary Battle, who was

slowly recovering from illness and would not have taken

LEFT: *At the side of Innisfree, Lough Gill.*
OVERLEAF: *Glencar lake, viewed from the east.*

the liberty) would go into fits of laughter. She believed I had spent the night in a different fashion and had invented the excuse to deceive my uncle, and would say to my great embarrassment, for I was as prudish as an old maid, *And you had good right to be fatigued.*"

From this youthful adventure one can trace the genealogy of some of Yeats' best loved verses, such as *The Lake Isle of Innisfree.* The sense of longing, the desire to find some peace amidst the still waters of Lough Gill, reflect the young exile's preoccupations. And certainly, he chose his isle of self-imposed solitude well. For the wooded shoreline of Lough Gill is still a magical place to wander. No matter whether you approach by the road that hugs the northern shore, passing the now reconstructed Parke's Castle (it was a romantic ruin in Yeats' day), or come from the southern side, looping around Slish Wood and then following the twisty road

LEFT: *St John's Church, Sligo in which Yeats' parents were married.*

marked "Innisfree", there are hidden corners and unexpected vistas to delight the eye. At the landing place are boats for hire, this being the only way to approach the small and densely wooded islet that Yeats called Innisfree, though local people also refer to it as "Cat Island." Some scholars even dispute whether this is indeed "The Lake Isle", though I was happy enough to do so, directing my curiosity more towards the lovely willow trees, the alder and the guelder rose, that flourish where woodland meets the water.

The landscape hereabouts is littered with place-names that appear in Yeats' earlier poems. Sometimes he changed their standard spelling, as in the opening lines of *The Stolen Child*, where Slish Wood becomes Sleuth Wood. Whatever the correct rendering, dense woods still rise dramatically from Lough Gill. And just to the west is Dooney Rock, upon which Yeats had his fiddler play folk dances. In ancient times a stone ring fort or cashel stood upon its

RIGHT: *Innisfree, Lough Gill.*

summit, commanding the valley through which the Garavogue River winds down towards Sligo Town and the sea. These days it is a nature reserve, within which rare exotica and indigenous species flourish. Apart from which, the views from Dooney Rock across Lough Gill and over towards Ben Bulben make this a rewarding climb, for the heart of Yeats' country is laid out before you.

If any place might challenge Lough Gill in W.B's affections, it is the smaller Glencar Lake which huddles beneath the mountains to the north. Yeats transports us there in *The Stolen Child*, along with the faery hosts, to a hidden spot of very special enchantment. This Glencar Waterfall – or, as Yeats would have it Glen-car – whose waters still plunge over a tree-shaded drop into "pools among the rushes / That scarce bathe a star". Unfortunately, these days the waterfall has become a popular attraction, and whatever poetry the

LEFT: *Woodlands detail.*

place once had is lost among "the unquiet dreams" of municipal planners who seem to take more joy in concrete walk-ways and car-parks than in preserving any spirit of place. To find something of what Yeats once saw, "leaning softly out / from ferns that drop their tears / over the young streams", it is best to wander beside one of the less celebrated streams that come rushing down into Lough Glencar; for there one can find true peace.

The visitor to Sligo will either welcome or resent the small brown plaques, adorned with pen and inkwell, which point the way to the next beauty spot with Yeatsian associations. I, for one, found them intrusive. Far more genuine was the ordinary black-and-white sign-post outside the churchyard at Drumcliff which points the way to Yeats United F.C. (football club). I do not know of any other literary figure who has a football club named after him; nor am I

RIGHT: *Yeats' football club.*

sure that W.B. – who was something of an aesthete – would have appreciated the honour. Nonetheless I took the turning, and passed by the modest football pitch where Sligo men must struggle against Atlantic gusts as well as the opposing team.

Not far west from here, and overlooking Drumcliff Bay, is Lissadell House, the spacious country seat of the Gore-Booth family. It was here that W.B., a townsman whose family fortunes were based on trade, encountered the more gracious ways of the landed gentry. Yeats was duly impressed by the "great sitting room as high as a church, and all things in good taste"; and the house is still there, the sitting room less stuffed with Victorian furniture but otherwise little changed.

Lissadell has been sensitively restored and is sometimes open to the public. I passed from room to room, stopping to admire the odd

LEFT: *View with reeds of Innisfree, Lough Gill.*

"Egyptian revival" fireplace and the full-size cartoons of family members and servants painted on the dining room walls. But probably the most famous feature in the house are the "great windows open to the south", in which Yeats recalls "two girls in silk kimonos, both / beautiful, one a gazelle". This poem dedicated to Eva Gore-Booth and her sister, Constance Markiewicz, was published after they were dead and is not exactly kind about their achievements – the one as a social reformer and trades unionist, the other as an Irish nationalist. Yeats rather scorned their activism – "all the folly of a fight with common wrong or right" – before concluding that "the innocent and the beautiful have no enemy but time".

It is an evocative place, Lissadell, with its history of forced clearances, its head-strong daughters, and its faded splendours. But for a first-hand experience of the 'ascendancy lifestyle', I treated

LEFT: *Constance Markievicz, (nee Gore-Booth) Major, Irish Citizen Army, 1916. Unveiled in St Stephen's Green, Dublin, 1956.*

myself to a ride through the park at Markree Castle, an imposing

mansion just south of Sligo which has been turned into a hotel and

riding centre. As we cantered past the park's broad-spreading

chestnuts and oak-trees I thought of Yeats, who wrote much about

his red pony but was so timorous a horseman. In that, at least, we

have something in common. My riding companion had been for

many years whipper-in with the Sligo Harriers, and he told me how

he had helped one of the Gore-Booth sisters, "who was mad about

horses but never been able to afford one until she was more than

seventy years old", to prepare a cob for the Dublin Horse Show.

Despite her age she left the ring with a prize. He also pointed out a

prehistoric ring fort, which the locals stayed clear of because they

believed the faeries lived there.

Stories of troubled spirits and ancient families become so entwined

around Sligo that I was not too surprised to hear that the spirit one

RIGHT: *Sculpture of Yeats in Sligo.*

of the Gore-Booths' ancestors is said to haunt the Derk of Knocklane, a deep cleft in the sea-cliffs beyond Lissadell. It is a wild and lonely place, open to the full fury of Atlantic storms; and it was here that Letitia Booth (who married Sir Nathaniel Gore) would roam dressed all in white, on one occasion forcing her coachman at gun-point to drive her around the cliff-edge. Since when her ghost is known as the Banshee Bawn, and her ghostly coach continues on its dizzying round, the carriage-horses shod with gold.

Below Knocklane Castle lies the village of Raughley, and behind that the Yellow Strand - another of W.B's favourite places. "I have walked on Sinbad's yellow shore", he wrote, "and never shall another's hit my fancy." From this windswept peninsula, the coast runs north and east to where the Spanish galleons foundered at Steedagh, and on to Mullaghmore, whose fine strands and peaceful fishing harbour belie the fact that this was where Lord Mountbatten was blown up.

LEFT: *Celtic Cross in St Columba's parish church, Drumcliffe.*
OVERLEAF: *Lissadell House.*

The coastline west of Sligo, past Cummeen Strand and on towards Strandhill, is less wild; and on a fine day presents superb views across the Channel and Coney Island (after which, it is believed, New York's Coney Island was named) to Rosses Point, with Ben Bulben rearing up behind. But when the wind and rain come sweeping in from Sligo Bay, the horizons close in and all grows menacing again, just as Yeats saw it in his poem *Red Hanrahan's song about Ireland*.

Continuing westward past Strandhill, the road passes directly beneath the great mound of Knocknarea, upon whose summit Queen Maeve is said to have had her throne installed. Yeats climbed up Knocknarea many times; but one occasion, when he and his cousins saw strange lights ascend the mountain, remained engraved on his mind.

RIGHT: *View of Classiebawn Castle, Sligo across bay.*

"That night, when I and my two cousins went for a walk, she saw the ground under some trees all in a blaze of light. I saw nothing, but presently we crossed the river and went along its edge where, they say, there was a village destroyed, I think in the wars of the seventeenth century, and near an old graveyard. Suddenly we all saw a light moving over the river where there is a great rush of waters. It was like a very brilliant torch. A moment later the girl saw a man coming towards us who disappeared in the water. I kept asking myself if I could be deceived. Perhaps after all, though it seemed impossible, somebody was walking in the water with a torch. But we could see a small light low down on Knocknarea seven miles off, and it began to move upward over the mountain slope. I timed it on my watch and in five minutes it reached the summit, and I, who had often climbed the mountain, knew that no human footstep was so speedy."

LEFT: *View from the churchyard, Drumcliff, where Yeats was buried.*

That supernatural experience, confirmed by his cousin's independent recollections, changed Yeats' life:

> "From that on I wandered about raths and faery hills and
> questioned old women and old men and, when I was tired
> out or unhappy, began to long for some such end as True
> Thomas found. I did not believe with my intellect that you
> could be carried away body and soul, but I believed with my
> emotions and the belief of the country people made
> that easy.

> And one night as I came near the village of Rosses on
> the road from Sligo, a fire blazed up on a green bank at my
> right side seven or eight feet above me, and another fire
> suddenly answered from Knocknarea. I hurried on
> doubting, and yet hardly doubting in my heart that I saw

RIGHT: *Late picture of WB Yeats.*

again the fires that I had seen by the river at Ballisodare. I began occasionally telling people that one should believe whatever had been believed in all countries and periods, and only reject any part of it after much evidence, instead of starting all over afresh and only believing what one could prove. But I was always ready to deny or turn into a joke what was for all that my secret fanaticism."

The seeds of that "secret fanaticism" had been implanted nearby, and much earlier on. For when still a young boy, he often went to stay at Ballisodare with his grand-uncle, William Middleton. And it was there he talked with the gardener, Paddy Flynn – "the most notable and typical story-teller of my acquaintance" – who lived in a cottage on the far side of the river. "Assuredly some joy not quite of this steadfast earth lightens in those eyes", wrote Yeats, "swift as the eyes of a rabbit among so many wrinkles, for Paddy Flynn is very old". And so young Willie would question Flynn. "Have you ever seen a faery?", he enquired. "Amn't I annoyed with them", replied the old man, who also said he had seen the banshee, "down there by the water 'batting' the river with its hands." The riverbanks are lined with osiers – known locally as 'salley rods' – making this the probable setting for his youthful poem, *Down by the Salley Gardens.*

The surrounding countryside around Ballisodare is echoed in poems written many decades later. The steep-sided valley, known locally as The Glen, most likely it was finds its way into the opening lines of *The Man and the Echo*:

> In a cleft that's christened Alt
>
> Under broken stone I halt
>
> At the bottom of a pit
>
> That broad noon has never lit,
>
> And shout a secret to the stone.
>
> All that I have said and done,
>
> Now that I am old and ill,

Turns into a question till

I lie awake night after night

And never get the answers right.

And certainly, if you take the narrow Glen Road that rises along the edge of Knocknarea, until you reach the cleft where rocks soar vertically on either side, and overhanging trees block out the sunlight, it seems certain this is the very place. Yeats had known of this "cleft", and been afraid of it since early childhood. As he recalls, "at Ballisodare there was a cleft among the rocks that I passed with terror because I believed that a murderous monster lived there that made a buzzing sound like a bee."

Across the River Ballisodore, I headed up a wooded lane towards The Hawk's Well, also known as Tubber Tullaghan and long respected for its magical qualities. From there I climbed high into the Ox Mountains, stopping at Ladies' Brae to look out over the whole natural amphitheatre, with Sligo Bay at its centre and bare-headed mountains guarding all the land approaches, which is the heart of Yeats' Country. A side road leads up into the Ox Mountains, with the Owenberg River rushing down from Lough Minnaun. This reedy lough, so popular with local anglers, is mentioned in the opening lines of *The Host of the Air* as 'the drear Hart Lake.'

Since I had already climbed Ben Bulben once, I excused myself from this essential stage in any Yeatsian pilgrimage. Instead I crossed the Dartry Mountains and entered the upland valley between Truskmore and Ben Bulben's back, on whose sheer rock face I saw the legendary Gleniff cave. It was here, the ancient story goes, that the lovers Diarmuid and Grainne were laid to rest, victims of the old and vengeful Fionn Mac Cumhail. The place is known as Diarmuid and Grainne's bed, and is adorned by fantastically shaped stalactites and stalagmites.

The whole area around Sligo is laden with ancient myths. Today, that same Celtic mythology serves Michael Quirke, a butcher-turned-woodcarver, as the subject matter for the statuettes he turns

ABOVE: *Farm buildings, Sligo.*

out, talking non-stop all the while, in the same premises where he once sold meat. "There was a time", he said, "when I combined the two, so there was carvings out in my shop window in between the chops and the offal. And why not?, I say, since there's no law against it. But these days I'm retired from the meat side of the business."

I noticed that among the mythological carvings there were some representations of old W.B.Yeats. "The visitors come in asking for it" he said, "and we get some peculiar visitors. Why, just the other day there was this druid from Canada, and with him a Mohawk Indian who played the Irish harp and drums. A stranger pair you could never imagine."

I wondered what the poet would have thought of these New Age dreamers, drawn by his writings and reputation half-way across the world to distant Sligo. Had they come to dream the same dream as his? For that is what tends to happen in Sligo. As Yeats' friend, the poet Arthur Symons, once said: "it is a place of dreams, a grey, gentle place, where the sand melts into the sea, the sea into the sky, and the mountains and clouds drift into one another." All that is still true of County Sligo; and long may it remain so.

II

DUBLIN

W B YEATS WAS A DUBLINER BY BIRTH. He passed the crucial years of his adolescence there. In later life, Dublin was the scene of some of his most notable triumphs, particularly in terms of founding a distinct tradition of Irish theatre which endures to this day. It was the scene of fierce literary arguments, of his personally confronting both the authorities and outraged mobs in the defence of his art. It was where he returned to, again and again, to look after "theatre business", or later on to speak as a Senator of the newly independent Ireland.

LEFT: *The Bank of Ireland.*

For all that, W.B had a distinctly ambivalent relationship with Dublin. He did not see its teeming city life as a source of inspiration for his writing, as James Joyce and others were to do. Instead he found there exposure to ideas, such as spiritualism and theosophy, which had come from elsewhere; or a very high-flown variety of Irish nationalism which fitted in with ideas already received. He saw Dublin as a platform from which to launch his own vision of an Irish literary revival. He sought an audience there. But one would be hard put to say he ever loved the place.

Although it is impossible to be certain, Yeats' earliest memories of "looking out of an Irish window at a wall covered with cracked and falling plaster" probably refer to Dublin. For it was there that he was born and spent the first three years of his life, the Yeats family then residing at a villa called "Georgeville" towards the end of Sandymount Avenue. In 1868, however, the Yeatses moved to

RIGHT: *WB Yeats' birthplace. 'Georgeville'.*
5 Sandymount Avenue, Dublin.

London, and it was not until young Willie was 15 years' old that they returned to Ireland on a more or less permanent basis. Initially they moved into "a long thatched house at Howth", just outside of Dublin. W.B tells us that:

> "Our house for the first year or so was on the top of a cliff, so that in stormy weather the spray would soak my bed at night, for I had taken the glass out of window, sash and all. A literary passion for the open air was to last me a few years. Then for another year or two we had a house overlooking the harbour where the one great sight was the going and coming of the fishing fleet. We had one regular servant, a fisherman's wife, and the occasional help of a big, red-faced girl who ate a whole pot of jam while my mother was at church and accused me of it."

LEFT: *Fishing boats at Howth.*

Yeats had a keen memory for the injustices of childhood. But he learned much from the long conversations his mother had with this fisherman's wife:

"When I think of her, I almost always see her talking over a cup of tea in the kitchen with our servant, the fisherman's wife, on the only themes outside the house that seemed of interest - the fishing-people of Howth, or the pilots and fishing people of Rosses Point. She read no books, but she and the fisherman's, wife would tell each other stories that Homer might have told, pleased with any moment of sudden intensity and laughing together over any point of satire."

RIGHT: *Moored boats on the river Liffey, Dublin.*

Howth and its environs provided a rich source of folk-lore and legend, for which young Willie had already developed a strong partiality when visiting his relatives in Sligo. For the woods around Howth were believed to be haunted by fairies, and by listening to such tales Yeats collected sufficient material for a whole chapter, entitled "Village Ghosts", to be included in *Celtic Twilight*, the first of his prose works which was published in 1893. His only regret was that "many a fine tale has been lost because it had not occurred to me soon enough to keep notes."

The sea-cliffs at Howth provided further opportunities for adventure – always taken alone, since the adolescent poet craved solitude and the intensity of experience it gave to him. He recalls how:

LEFT: *Sea Shore at Howth.*

"A herd had shown me a cave some hundred and fifty feet below the cliff path and a couple of hundred feet above the sea, and told me that an evicted tenant called Macrom, dead some fifteen years, had lived there many years, and shown me a rusty nail in the rock which had served perhaps to hold some wooden protection from wind and weather. Here I stored a tin of cocoa and some biscuits, and instead of going to bed, would slip out on warm nights and sleep in the cave on the excuse of catching moths. One had to pass over a rocky ledge, safe enough for any one with a fair head, yet seeming, if looked at from above, narrow and sloping; and a remonstrance from a stranger who had seen me climbing along it doubled my delight in the adventure."

With its pretty fishing port shielded by the cliffs from the worst of the weather, Howth still makes a popular outing for Dubliners these days – whether or not they end up, like "the bank holiday lovers", in one of Yeats' chosen caves. "At other times", he tells us;

ABOVE: *South wall bay, Dublin.*

"I would sleep among the rhododendrons and rocks in the wilder part of the grounds of Howth Castle. After a while my father said I must stay indoors half the night, meaning that I should get some sleep in my bed; but I, knowing that I would be too sleepy and comfortable to get up again, used to sit over the kitchen fire till half the night was gone. Exaggerated accounts spread through the school, and sometimes when I did not know a lesson some master would banter me about the way my nights were spent."

The school he was now attending in Dublin was the Erasmus High School, which is still there in Harcourt Street. Each morning he would take the train into Dublin with his father, whose artist's studio was near to St Stephen's Green, one of the main hubs of Dublin's Anglo-Irish society.

"My father's influence upon my thoughts was at its height. We went to Dublin by train every morning, breakfasting in his studio. He had taken a large room with a beautiful eighteenth-century mantelpiece in a York Street tenement-house, and at breakfast he read passages from the poets, and always from the play or poem at its most passionate moment."

Already the young W.B. was seeking a voice with which to articulate his adolescent passions and visions of beauty. The

RIGHT: *Ardilaun Lodge, Harcourt Entrance of St Stephen's Green Park.*

influence of his artistic father may have steered him towards a poetic vocation, but it did little to improve his school record. Unlike previous generations of Yeatses, W.B. was not of a sufficiently scholarly bent to gain admittance to Trinity College, Dublin. "My father had wanted me to go to Trinity College, and when I would not, had said, 'My father and grandfather and great-grandfather have been there'. I did not tell him that neither my classics nor my mathematics were good enough for any examination." Perhaps this was just as well, for the living his father made from portrait painting could scarcely have covered the expense.

The Yeats family moved closer into Dublin, to the more suburban surroundings of 10 Ashfield Terrace (now 418 Harold's Cross Road) in Rathgar. W.B. was not that impressed. "We lived in a villa", he recalled, "where the red bricks were made pretentious and

LEFT: *Grafton Street, 1904*

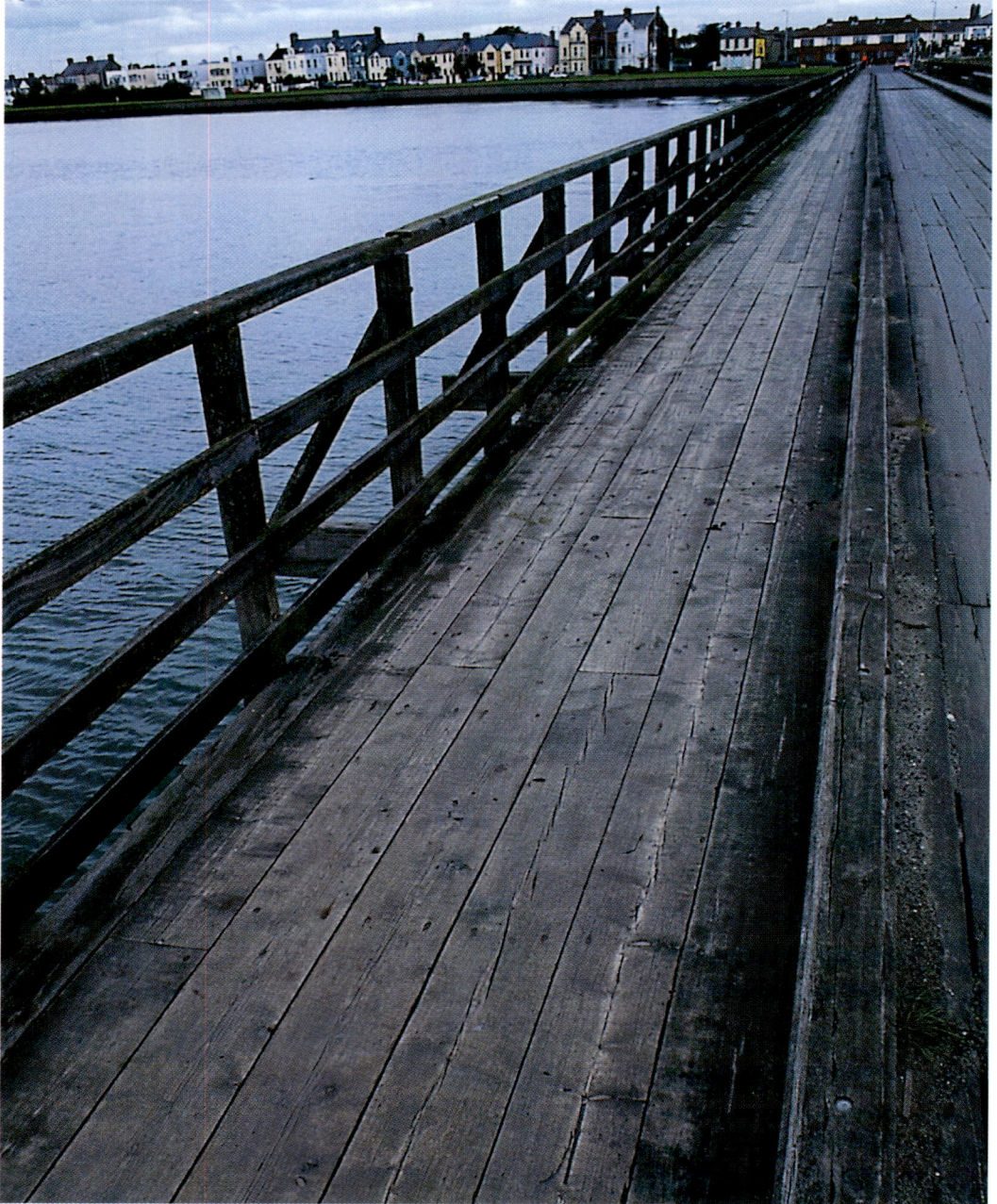

vulgar with streaks of slate colour, and there seemed to be enemies everywhere." Or again, "that Rathgar villa where we all lived when I went to school, a time of crowding and indignity." Partly this distaste for his new surroundings stemmed from W.B's innate snobbery, partly from his aversion to all that was modern and ugly. Rathgar was respectable enough in a modest way; but it fell outside the main bastions of Anglo-Irish society: the Georgian houses and the clubs around St Stephen's Green; the National Library; and, of course, Trinity College, to which Yeats might well have felt he rightly belonged. He treasured the many visits with his father to see Edward Dowden, the Poet and Professor of English Literature at Trinity College, whose house on Temple Road was definitely a step up in the world.

LEFT: *The crossing at Dollymount.*

"From our first arrival in Dublin, my father had brought me from time to time to see Edward Dowden. He and my father had been college friends and were trying, perhaps, to take up again their old friendship. Sometimes we were asked to breakfast and my father would would tell me to read out one of my poems. Dowden was wise in his encouragement, never overpraising and never unsympathetic, and he would sometimes lend me books. The orderly, prosperous house where all was in good taste, where poetry was rightly valued, made Dublin tolerable for a while."

But there other causes of anxiety. The future poet was going through all the awkwardness of adolescence. That "great event of a boy's life...the awakening of sex" had already occurred "like the

RIGHT: *The interior of St Patrick's church.*

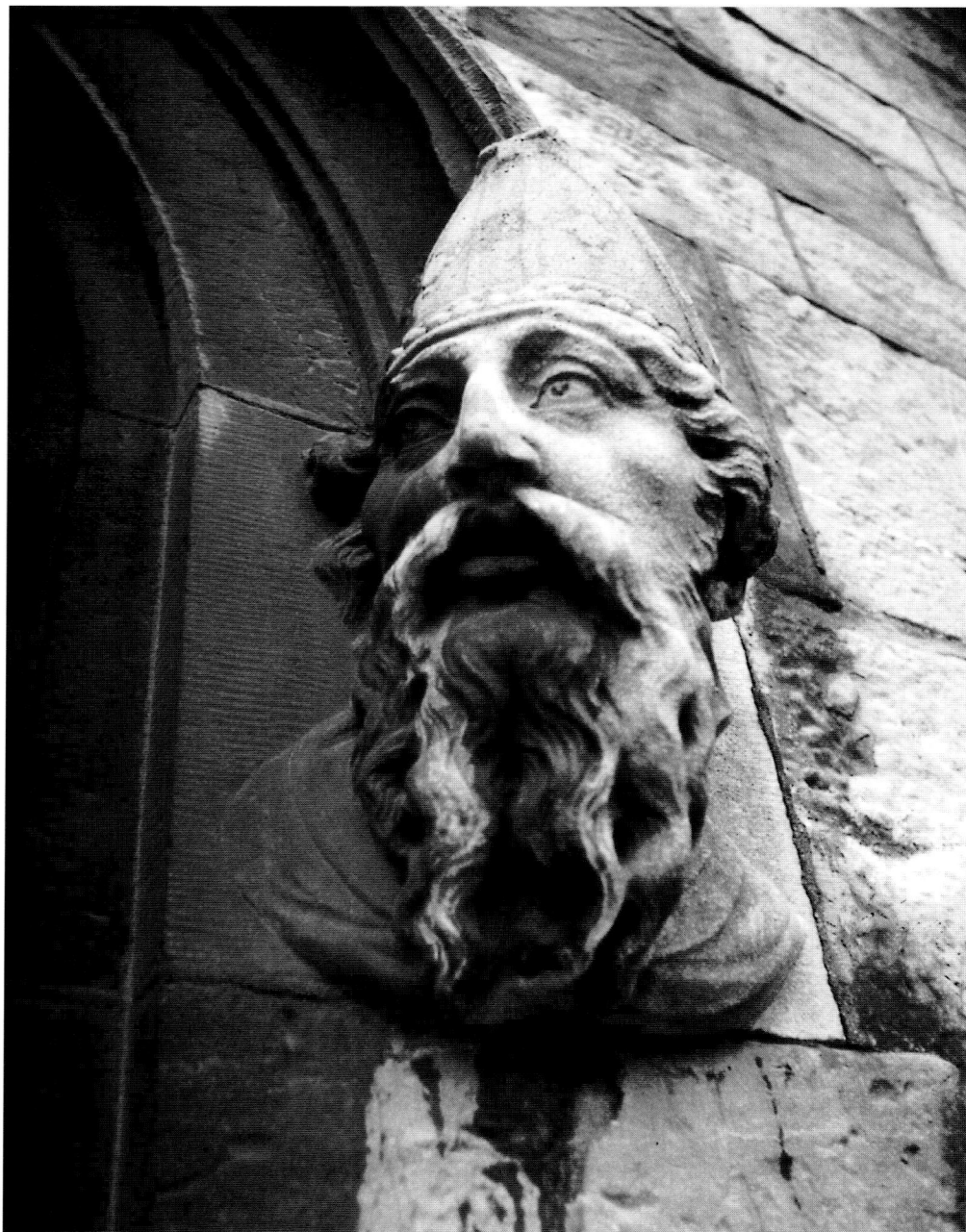

bursting of a shell" when he was living at Howth. And it was there he spotted the first girl he would fall for, a distant cousin of the Yeatses called Laura Armstrong.

> "I was climbing up a hill at Howth when I heard wheels behind me and a pony-carriage drew up beside me. A pretty girl was driving alone without a hat. She told me her name and said we had friends in common and asked me to ride with her. After that I saw a great deal of her and was soon in love. I did not tell her I was in love , however, because she was engaged."

Sadly for Yeats, she married soon afterwards. None of which exactly bolstered his self-confidence. For despite his attractiveness to women, his pale olive skin and shock of black hair, he was terribly self-conscious.

LEFT: *Dublin Castle relief.*

ABOVE: *Trinity College in the late 19th century.*
LEFT: *Trinity College today.*

The college was founded in 1591 by Elizabeth I on the site of a monastery. Most of the buildings date from the 18th century.

Trinity was at the time of Yeats still a Protestant university. Only in the last 30 years have Catholics attended in large numbers. The Republic's Protestant population has shrunk from 20% at the time of partition to only 2% today.

Much later in life he would recall how he walked the streets "with an artful stride in memory of Hamlet", and of how "the policeman and tramway conductor thought my absence of mind sufficiently explained when our servant told them I was a poet. 'O, well' said the policeman, who had been asking why I went indifferently through clean and muddy places, 'if it is only the poetry that is working in his head!'" Perhaps he played the absent-minded poet, waving his arms as he beat out some unformulated rhyme, a little too seriously for the Dubliners he encountered, for they are generally endowed with a great talent for debunking. It was for him a time of dreadful insecurities, as he himself recognised some 40 years later.

RIGHT: *The Dáil.*

ABOVE: *Custom House, 19th century.*
RIGHT: *Custom House today. It was, commissioned by John Beresford, the greatly hated First Commissioner of the Revenue (i.e. colonial taxman-in-chief) and designed by Gandon. Completed in 1791, it was immediately recognised as a masterpiece and one contemporary writer remarked: 'It is in every aspect a noble edifice, in which there is no fault to be found, except that old Beresford is sumptuously lodged in it.' It was the major centre for British power in Ireland for 130 years, until it was gutted by fire in 1921, during the War of Independence. When it was restored under the new Irish government, the interior was radically altered and the central dome was rebuilt in grey Ardbraccan stone from County Meath, rather than the original white Portland stone from Dorset, Southern England. Gandon went on to design O'Connell Bridge and the eastern portico of Parliament House (Bank of Ireland).*

"I am always thinking of myself at that age", he wrote, "the age I was when my father painted me a King Goll, tearing the strings out of a harp, being insane with youth, but looking very desirable – alas no woman noticed it at the time – with dreamy eyes and a great mass of black hair. It hangs in our drawing room now – a pathetic memory of a really dreadful time."

The straitened financial circumstances in which the Yeats family lived did nothing to boost W.B.'s confidence.

"I used to imagine I looked gaunt and emaciated, for the little boys at the neighbouring cross-roads used to say when I passed by: 'O, here is King Death again'."

And money was certainly tight:

RIGHT: *The old city gate S. Audoen's arch.*

"I had very little money and one day the toll-taker at
the metal bridge over the Liffey and a gossip of his laughed
when I refused the half-penny and said, 'No, I will go
around by O'Connell Bridge.' When I called for the first
time at a house in Leinster Road several middle-aged
women were playing cards and suggested my talking a
hand and gave me glass of sherry. The sherry went to my
head and I was impoverished for days by the loss
of sixpence."

Likewise, his sister Lily recalled having to walk in from Rathgar to college because there was no money to pay the tram fares. Meanwhile, W.B's schooling had been transferred to the Metropolitan School of Art in Kildare Street, where his father was a master and the fees were low.

LEFT: *Ha'penny Bridge (1816)*
So named after the toll that was charged for crossing it and Yeats tried to avoid paying.

For all that, Yeats' internal life was developing apace. He was writing more poetry now, and it was in the Dublin University Review that two of his poems were first published in 1885. In and around Dublin, he was meeting writers and thinkers who were to have a profound influence on him in later life. One of his fellow art students was a mystical fellow called George Russell who preferred to be known simply as AE and was to be the closest of Yeats' friends. And it was in the house where W.B took too much sherry and lost sixpence at cards that he met the Fenian leader John O'Leary, "the handsomest old man I had ever seen." But far more than that, "from O'Leary's conversation and from the Irish books he lent or gave me has come all that I have set my hand to since." A profound influence, then, and a helping hand: for it was John O'Leary who helped in finding subscribers that made possible the publication of Yeats' first book of poems. Under this same roof, W.B encountered such figures as

RIGHT: *Monument to James Clarence Mangan (1803-1849) in St Stephen's Green. He was called by some the greatest poet of the 19th century. He died of cholera. This piece was the last work of Willie Pearce, who was executed in 1916 because of his involvement in the Easter uprising.*

Dr Douglas Hyde, who had recently founded the Gaelic League to further the use of the Irish language. He also met the great nationalist orator John Taylor, and the poetess Katharine Tynan who took him to his first séance.

Yeats became even more absorbed in spiritualism and mystical explorations after his family moved back to London, where he met Madame Blavatsky and joined the Theosophical Society. But even then he was working on Irish material. In 1887 his edition of *Poems and Ballads of Young Ireland* was published in Dublin. The following year, he compiled a volume of *Fairy and Folk Tales of the Irish Peasantry*. He was beginning to earn a reputation both as a poet and an authority on Irish folk-lore; and in London he founded the Irish Literary Society and met such notable Irish literary emigrés as Oscar Wilde and George Bernard Shaw. He also met and fell in love with the beautiful Maud Gonne, who almost certainly

LEFT: *Oscar Wilde.*

provided the inspiration for the title role in his first play, *The Countess Cathleen*. When this was first performed in Dublin it caused something of a scandal, the story of a beautiful noblewoman who sold her soul to the Devil to save poor villagers from starving being deemed theologically unsound. Maud Gonne, however, did not return the poet's adoration, and married instead the nationalist hero Captain John MacBride.

Yeats passed through Dublin almost every year, to sort out business with his publishers, to meet up with old friends, to try and establish Dublin as the natural centre of his Irish Literary Society, or simply to await the arrival of the ever-elusive Maud Gonne. But he always moved on, to see his relations in Sligo, or increasingly to visit Lady Gregory at Coole Park in County Galway. And it was there that the seeds of his most enduring enterprise, the creation of an Irish Literary Theatre, were sown.

RIGHT: *Portrait of Yeats on Sandymount Green.*

However, the natural locus for this movement to revive Irish and Celtic drama was Dublin, and the very first performances were held in 1899 at the Ancient Concert Rooms in Molesworth Street, with Yeats' *The Countess Cathleen* sharing the billing with Edward Martyn's *The Heather Field*. From those early tumultuous days, when Yeats' play provoked audiences to barrages of protest and counter-demonstration, a direct line can be drawn to the founding in 1904 of the Abbey Theatre, whose more modern successor still stands in Abbey Street.

But the way was not smooth. For its second season, the Irish Literary Theatre staged two more of Edward Martyn's plays, one of them extensively re-written by W.B's fellow art school student, George Moore. Yeats and Moore also collaborated on a play based

LEFT: *Lion, part of the Rutland memorial fountain, 1791, opposite the National Gallery of Ireland, Merrion Square, west side.*

on the ancient legend of Diarmuid and Grania, a version of which was produced the Gaiety Theatre in Dublin. In order to reduce the reliance on English actors, the brothers Frank and William Fay were brought in to train up a company of Irish players, and in 1902 Yeats' patriotic *Cathleen ni Houlihan* was staged in St Teresa's Hall with Maud Gonne in the leading role.

But by now some of the original founders of the Irish Literary Theatre had resigned. So a new venture was begun, the Irish National Theatre, with Yeats himself as President and with invaluable backing from the English impresario and patron of the theatre, Miss A.E.Horniman, who helped first to stage Yeats' new play, *The King's Threshold*, and then funded the transformation of two buildings in Abbey Street into the Abbey Theatre.

RIGHT: *Statue of Daniel O'Connell, 19th century leader of constitutional nationalism.*

The Abbey opened its doors on 27 December, 1904, with productions of Yeats' *On Baile's Strand, Cathleen ni Houlihan,* and Lady Gregory's *Spreading the News.* While W.B. spent more time in Dublin, it was mainly on "theatre business" – dealing with the authorities in Dublin Castle on such matters as theatre patents, personally supervising the theatrical effects and lighting for his own works, or giving interviews and showing the press over the new theatre. And it is more of literary and theatrical matters that he writes, not of the city of Dublin as such. And yet it was so pivotal in Yeats' life, the only city in which his dreams of an Irish literary renaissance could really take form. Dublin was for him like a battlefield, where one moment he must fight against wilful obscurantism, the next against the flippancy or plain philistinism of a provincial press – "our base half-men of letters, or rather half-journalists", as he calls them. It was where both his most vicious detractors and ardent supporters congregated. All these passions

LEFT: *Prime Minister Gladstone debating 'the Irish question' in 1886.*

broke out during the riots which attended the staging of J.M.Synge's

The Playboy of the Western World, which Yeats recognised as a

dramatic masterpiece but which many felt was derogatory about

Ireland and the Irish character.

A young devotee of Yeats, Mary Collum, was present at that

turbulent performance.

LEFT: *St George's Church, mid 18th century.*
ABOVE: *19th century view of Post Office in Sackville Street,*
now called O'Connell Street.

"A motley mixture of workmen, students, and bourgeoisie in evening dress filled the theatre, most of them with denunciatory speeches ready to deliver. Yeats took the platform in full evening dress and faced the crowd. Step by step he interpreted the play, delivering in the process some of his complex theories of art, one moment cowing the audience, the next shouted down by them ...

Even on the patriotics Yeats was equal to them, 'The author

ABOVE: *Charles Stuart Parnell (1846-91) and Kitty O'Shea.*
RIGHT: *Parnell addressing his constituents from a window of
the Victoria Hotel in Cork.*

Lighting on O'Connell Bridge.

of *Cathleen Ni Houlihan* addresses you', he said.

The audience, remembering that passionately patriotic play,

forgot its antagonism for a few moments and Yeats got his

cheers. ... I never witnessed a human being fight as Yeats

fought that night, nor knew another with so many weapons

in his armoury."

And Dubliners should be thankful that this man, seemingly so timid, was ready to stand up and fight for what he believed in.   For it was in large part due to Yeats' single-minded determination that Dublin grew into a city where the performing arts can flourish - as they do to this day. Not that he was always confident that his work in the theatre would survive long. Just two years after *The Playboy* was first staged, W.B wrote in despondent mood:

"The Abbey Theatre will fail to do its full work because there is no accepted authority why the more difficult pleasure is the nobler pleasure."

His disenchantment with popular theatre was already well set in. Another blow came with the withdrawal of Miss Horniman's support when she discovered that, by mischance, the Abbey's usual evening performance went ahead on the day of King Edward VII's death. Fortunately by now the Abbey Theatre was sufficiently well-established to continue without this support. But Yeats' interest shifted towards a more stylised and exacting repertoire, and he began writing in the manner of Japanese *Noh* theatre. He retreated into a more private world, where the silent and masked figures of *Plays for Dancers* might perform before some select private audience – scarce dreaming that 20 years later this same play would be staged at The Abbey Theatre with the choreography by Ninette de Valois.

From his early involvement in the Young Ireland movement, Yeats had always considered himself as an Irish patriot. And yet, he developed his own idealised concept of what it meant to be a nationalist which, as the storm clouds gathered, became further and further removed from the sentiments of most of his fellow countrymen.

RIGHT: *Old style shop front.*

St Patrick's Cathedral.

He himself seems to acknowledge this in his poem *September 1913*:

"Romantic Ireland's dead and gone,

It's with O'Leary in the grave."

Perhaps it was his family background that left him feeling he had a foot in both camps. Or perhaps his natural tendency to aloofness kept him at arm's length from the rough-and-tumble of Dublin politics around the turn of the century. Even when his beloved Maud Gonne is at the centre of the action – as during the protests over Queen Victoria's Jubilee – Yeats seems to observe as if from some distant tower.

> "The meeting is held in College Green and is very crowded, and Maud Gonne speaks, I think, standing upon a chair. Maud Gonne tells how that morning she had gone to lay a wreath upon a martyr's tomb at Saint Michael's Church, for it is the one day in the year when such wreaths are laid, but had been refused admission because it is the Jubilee. Then she pauses, and after that her voice rises to a cry, 'Must the graves of our dead go undecorated because Victoria has her Jubilee?'"

And when, shortly afterwards, Queen Victoria visited Dublin to be cheered by the children of Unionists, while over beyond Drumcondra thousands more children are marshalled by Maud

Gonne and made to swear undying enmity towards England - all this causes the poet to ask: "How many of these children will carry a bomb or rifle when a little under or a little over the age of thirty?"

From here one can trace Yeats' disenchantment with populist or revolutionary politics which led him, in old age, to write such bitter poems as *The Great Day;*

> HURRAH for revolution and more cannon-shot!
> A beggar upon horseback lashes a beggar on foot.
> Hurrah for revolution and cannon come again !
> The beggars have changed places, but the lash goes on.

Yet when, during Easter Week of 1916, the Irish Republican volunteers rose up and occupied the General Post Office in

RIGHT: *19th century view of the law courts.*

O'Connell Street, the sheer heroism of these men inspired Yeats to write what is surely one of his finest poems, *Easter 1916*. The thrice-repeated final line, the roll-call of the nationalist leaders executed for their part in the Easter Rising, achieve a dreadful solemnity.

We know their dream; enough

To know they dreamed and are dead;

And what if excess of love

Bewildered them till they died?

I write it out in a verse-

MacDonagh and MacBride

And Connolly and Pearse

Now and in time to be,

Wherever green is worn,

Are changed, changed utterly:

A terrible beauty is born.

LEFT: *19th century view of the Royal Exchange.*

The General Post Office was shelled to smithereens; but to visit the building erected in its place with those verses in mind remains a deeply moving experience. And it is fitting that the page with this poem should be kept open at the Dublin Writers' Museum in Parnell Square.

The following year Yeats married, and henceforth spent more time in England or down in County Galway. His visits to Dublin tended to be brief and business-like. "I had come to Dublin for a few days to see about Abbey business", he wrote to Olivia Shakespear. Then, with Ireland on the brink of civil war, the Yeats family moved into the fine Georgian house he had bought in Merrion Square, Dublin. The new Free State Government offered him a seat in the Irish Senate, which he took up early in 1923, becoming -as he himself put it - the "sixty-year-old smiling public man". He took his public duties seriously, preparing speeches on

George Bernard Shaw, 1890s

copyright and the coinage. But by the late 1920s he was suffering

from lung congestion, and from then on he often passed the winters

in Italy or elsewhere in the Mediterranean.

OVERLEAF: *Dublin's Post Office.*

The last Irish house that Yeats lived in was 'Riversdale', near the village of Rathfarnham. It lies between Dublin and the mountains, allowing easy access to the city. The old poet would still occasionally drop in at the Abbey Theatre. Otherwise he kept to himself, enjoying the gardens around his house where "plum and cabbage grew". Increasingly at odds with the world around him, he decried what he saw as the bogus sentimentalism of modern life. He even had a brief fling with fascism. And Dubliners often mocked him for his oddities, his supernatural leanings, his wilful obscurantism. But mostly they recognised him for what he was - a singular individual and one of Ireland's greatest poets. Long after his death, when his mortal remains finally returned to Ireland, all of Dublin came out to pay their respects.

RIGHT: *O'Connell's statue in O'Connell Street.*

III

GALWAY

IT MIGHT SEEM impossible that any place could supersede Sligo in Yeats' affections. But if such a place ever did exist, it is almost certainly Coole Park in County Galway. For it was to this great house, surrounded by woodlands and lakes, that he withdrew to write and reflect over thirty summers and many winters besides. It was here that he found the romantic ruin of a medieval tower that he chose to have restored as his home in later, married life. And certainly, this forgotten corner of south-west Galway has all the requisite qualities of a writer's retreat.

LEFT AND OVERLEAF: *The entrance to Coole Park.*

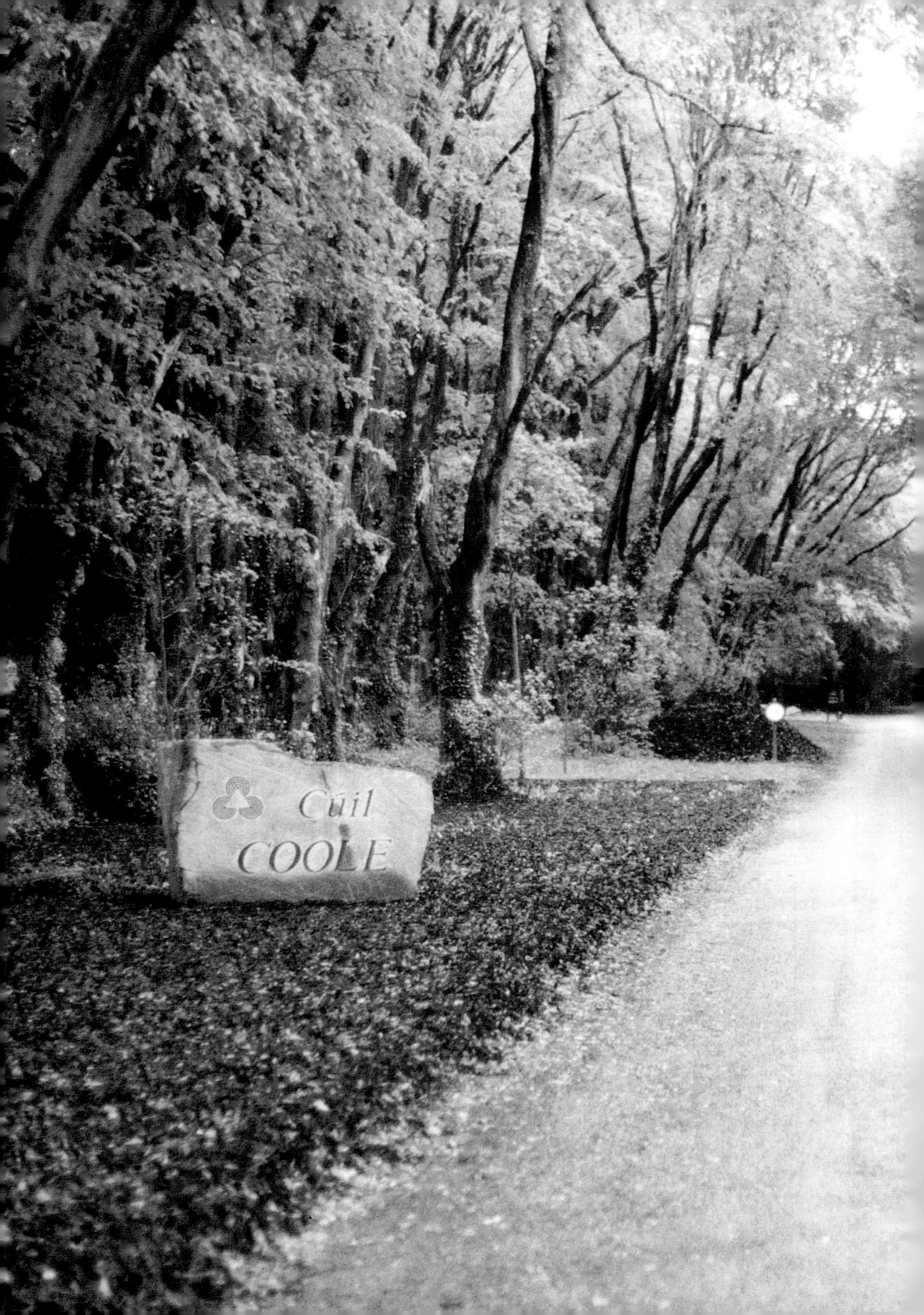
Cúil
COOLE

Even today, with the assistance of little brown-painted plaques pointing the way, it is not easy to find Coole Park. Indeed, once I had turned off the main Galway-Limerick road and onto the narrow, single track country lanes that wind their way between flowering hedgerows and lush pastures, I became utterly lost. Or at least I had the impression of being lost until there appeared, as if out of nowhere, a fine avenue flanked by over-arching ilex trees. That I had definitely arrived at Coole Park was confirmed by a large sign carved in stone; but quite how I got there I'll never know.

The path that led W.B. Yeats to Coole Park can be seen as even more of a happy coincidence. He had travelled over to Ireland in 1896 with his collaborator on *The Savoy* magazine, Arthur Symons. After visiting Sligo and Aran together, they went down to Galway

LEFT: *Ruins within Coole Park.*

to visit a mutual friend, Edward Martyn, at his country seat of Tulira Castle. Yeats recalled that when he had met Martyn in London, "he had seemed so heavy, uncouth, countrified that I said as we turned in at the gate: 'We shall be waited on by a barefoot servant."

It was while staying at Tulira Castle – "perhaps after Arthur Symons had gone" – that the châtellaine of Coole, the redoubtable Lady Augusta Gregory, made a neighbourly call and "reminded me that we had met in London though but for a few minutes at some fashionable house." The upshot of their meeting again was an invitation to come over to Coole Park for lunch. It was the beginning of a long and extremely important relationship for Yeats. Lady Gregory was to become his firmest friend, his counsellor, patroness, and literary collaborator – though possibly the greatest of her many benefactions was simply to open to Yeats the hospitality

RIGHT: *Cover of Savoy magazine, designed and illustrated by Aubrey Beardsley.*
OVERLEAF: *One of the rare photographs of Coole Park House, the west front, 1887.*

THE SAVOY

AUBREY
BEARDSLEY.
1896.

of Coole Park. In time, that house was to become the nerve-centre of the Irish Literary Revival. And in time, Yeats came "to love that house more than all other houses."

From the very outset it made a deep impression. "A glimpse of a long vista of trees, over an undergrowth of clipped laurels, seen for a moment as the outside car approached her house on my first visit, is a vivid memory."

As for the house itself, it "was plain and box-like, except on the side towards the lake, where somebody...had enlarged the drawing-room and dining-room with great bow windows." Of this ancient house – which, as Yeats pointed out, pre-dated the return of architecture in Georgian times – hardly a stone remains standing today; so all that one finds at the end of the tree-lined avenue are the foundations. The decision to demolish Coole Park

LEFT: *Detail of the ruins of Coole Park House.*

ABOVE: *Plaque at Coole Park*
RIGHT: *Fallen tree at Coole Park.*

was taken in 1941, with government approval, and it was only much more recently that efforts have been made to retrieve something of its vanished glory by building up the foundations and converting the barn and stables into a Visitor's Centre.

With the house irretrievably gone, what now draws the visitor on are the surrounding woodlands (much replenished since the days when W.B regretted the cutting down of so many ancient trees in the park). For Yeats, the woods around Coole acquired a very special, even mystical, significance which made him prize them even above the much-loved woods of Sligo.

"Certain woods at Sligo, ... though I shall never perhaps walk there again, are so deep in my affections that I dream about them at night; and yet the woods at Coole, though they do not come into my dream, are so much more

RIGHT: *Cricketing legend WG Grace was said to be a visitor to Coole Park, although the locals said that it was less for the cricket matches that were held in the park, more for the out-of-season shooting.*

knitted to my thought that when I am dead they will have,

I am persuaded, my longest visit."

And it was here, at Coole, that his dream-world merged with his
waking experiences, his absorption in Celtic myth and paganism
leading him through strange paths to something akin to a Christian
mystical experience: Yeats describes it in these terms:

"I was crossing a little stream near Inchy Wood and
actually in the middle of a stride from bank to bank, when
an emotion never experienced before swept down upon
me. I said, 'That is what the devout Christian feels, that is
how he surrenders his will to the will of God'. I felt an
extreme surprise, for my whole imagination was
preoccupied with the pagan mythology of ancient Ireland, I
was marking in red ink, upon a large map, every sacred
mountain. The next morning I awoke near dawn, to hear a

RIGHT: *Cottage by the side of the Poets Cemetery, Killeeneen.*

ABOVE AND NEXT TWO PHOTOGRAPHS: *Coole Lough*

voice saying, 'The love of God is infinite for every human soul because every human soul is unique; no other can satisfy the same need in God'.

The most constant source of enchantment at Coole, however, was (and still is) its lake. To find this, you follow the path that leads down from the right-hand side of the foundations. Eventually this brings you to to Coole Lough. Here Yeats would go to walk alone and brood on as yet imperfectly-formed verses. Here he would sometimes sketch, or take a boat out on the lake with literary friends down from Dublin, with a picnic tea to follow. "In later years", he wrote, "I was to know the edges of that lake better than any spot on earth, to know it in all the changes of the seasons, to find there always some new beauty."

It was by these still waters that Yeats' possessive love of landscape was unleashed to form images which then, with infinite patience and much toil, he refined into one of his best-loved poems, *The Wild Swans at Coole:*

THE WILD SWANS AT COOLE

The trees are in their autumn beauty,

The woodland paths are dry,

Under the October twilight the water

Mirrors a still sky;

Upon the brimming water among the stones

Are nine-and-fifty swans.

The nineteenth autumn has come upon me

Since I first made my count;

I saw, before I had well finished,

All suddenly mount

And scatter wheeling in great broken rings

Upon their clamorous wings.

I have looked upon these brilliant creatures,

And now my heart is sore.

All's changed since I, hearing at twilight,

The first time on this shore,

The bell-beat of their wings above my head,

Trod with a lighter tread.

Unwearied still, lover by lover,

They paddle in the cold

Companionable streams or climb the air;

Their hearts have not grown old;

Passion or conquest, wander where they will,

Attend upon them still.

But now they drift on the still water,

Mysterious, beautiful;

Among what rushes will they build,

By what lake's edge or pool

Delight men's eyes when I awake some day

To find they have flown away?

The seasons may have changed, the swans scattered; and yet, to sit silently beside Coole Lough, and see the measured beauty of those lines reflected in a landscape that is so little altered since Yeats' day, is reason enough to journey to this hidden corner of Galway.

Further memories are literally engraved upon the smooth trunk of the copper beech which towers above all other trees around it. For it was the habit of guests to Coole Park carve their initials in the bark, or have them carved for them. On one occasion, at least, W.B took on the task of carving the initials. In 1901 it was Violet Martin's turn, as she recounted to her cousin.

"Today Augusta (Lady Gregory) made me add my initials to a tree already decorated by Douglas Hyde, AE (George Russell) and more of the literary crowd. It was most touching. W.B. Yeats did the carving, I smoked, and high literary conversation raged and the cigarette went out and I couldn't make the matches light, and he held out the little lappets of his coat and I lighted the match in his bosom. No one was there, and I trust no one saw, as it must have looked very funny".

Those visiting Coole Park may find this tree beyond the old garden wall; and Yeats' own initials are up there still, though difficult to discern these days since so many others have added their own graffiti.

This habit, of having a "living guest book", was typical of Lady Augusta Gregory. Already seven years a widow when she first met Yeats, Lady Gregory was born into a prominent county family, the

Persses, who had settled in Galway during the 17th century. She grew up at Roxborough House, which once stood beside the road from Gort to Loughrea, and at the age of 29 married the scion of another county family, Sir William Gregory, a much older man who took her with him to India and Ceylon where he was the colonial governor. Yeats describes her thus:

"Lady Gregory, as I first knew her, was a plainly dressed woman of forty-five, without obvious good looks, except the charm that comes from strength, intelligence and kindness. One who knew her at an earlier date speaks of dark skin, of extreme vitality, and a portrait by Mrs. Jopling that may have flattered shows considerable beauty. When her husband died, she had given up her London house, had devoted herself to the estate and to her son, spending little that mortgages might be paid off. The house had become her passion. That passion grew greater still when the house took its place in the public life of Ireland.'

When Yeats and Edward Martyn first met Lady Gregory at Tulira Castle, both were working on new plays – Yeats on *The Countess Cathleen*, Martyn on *The Heather Field*. Lady Gregory also had a lively interest in the dramatic arts, and in due course was to write her own play, *The Rising of the Moon*. From that chance meeting grew the idea of establishing the Irish Literary Theatre; though the real discussion had to await the following year. It took place at a friend's house, as Yeats himself records:

> "On the sea-coast at Duras, a few miles from Coole, an old French Count, Florimond de Basterot, lived for certain months in every year. Lady Gregory and I talked over my project of an Irish Theatre, looking out upon the lawn of his house, watching a large flock of ducks that was always gathered for his arrival from Paris. I told her that I had given up my project because it was impossible to get the few

pounds necessary for a start in little halls, and she promised to collect or give the money necessary. That was her first great service to the Irish intellectual movement."

And many others besides Yeats - scholars, artists and politicians – were inspired by Lady Gregory and the intellectual ferment of her rustic salon at Coole Park. "If that influence were lacking", he wrote, "Ireland would have been greatly impoverished, so much has been planned out in the library or among the woods at Coole." Yeats' own literary output would likewise been greatly impoverished were it not for Lady Gregory's constantly pushing him to further activity. Poet and patron shared consuming interest in Irish folk-lore and when, as in the summer of 1897, W.B found himself incapable of work, she took him on literary expeditions around the local cottages.

"Finding that I could not work, and thinking the open air salutary, Lady Gregory brought me from cottage to cottage collecting folk-lore. Every night she wrote out what we had heard in the dialect of the cottages. She wrote, if my memory does not deceive me, two hundred thousand words, discovering that vivid English she was the first to use upon the stage. My object was to find actual experience of the supernatural, for I did not believe, nor do I now, that it is possible to discover in the text-books of the schools, in the manuals sold by religious booksellers, even in the subtle reverie of saints, the most violent force in history."

For Yeats it was like entering into another world. "When we passed the door of some peasant's cottage, we passed out of Europe as that word is understood". From such conversations he acquired much fascinating material, which influenced his own spiritual experiences and, he believed, deeply influenced the development of his own character. As he explains it;

"Lady Gregory and I had heard many tales of changelings, grown men and woman as well as children, who, as the people believe, are taken by the faeries, some spirit or inanimate object bewitched into their likeness remaining in their stead, and I constantly asked myself what reality there could be in these tales, often supported by so much testimony. I woke one night to find myself lying upon my back with all my limbs rigid, and to hear a ceremonial measured voice, which did not seem to be mine, speaking through my lips. 'We make an image of him who sleeps', it said, 'and it is not he who sleeps, and we call it Emmanuel'. After many years that thought, others often found as strangely being added to it, because the thought of the Mask, which I have used in these memoirs to explain men's characters."

Mystical resonances and astrology also had much to do with Yeats' decision to marry George Hyde-Lees and set up house within

'Thoor Ballylee', the keep of a Norman castle some five miles'
distance from Coole Park. Yeats had spotted it many years earlier,
and was instinctively attracted to the place. But being still a
bachelor, he thought living in this high tower by himself would be
too much. He decided to postpone any decision as to Tur Bail i
Laigh – to give it its true, Gaelic name – until after he was married.

The Yeatses moved into the tower in 1919, and it remained their
summer home for more than ten years. But for the poet, Thoor
Ballylee was more than a retreat conveniently close to Lady
Gregory's literary menagerie at Coole Park. The tower became for
him a symbol of all that "the great and passionate" had done in the
past, and of how he strove to preserve that heritage for the future –
despite the possible intervention of planners from government
offices upon whom the poet casts a warning shot of a curse in his
poem *A Prayer on Going Into My House.*

For Yeats' cyclical vision of history meant that all would return to ruin. But almost in defiance of that inevitability, he had inscribed upon a stone these verses, with which he dedicated is Thoor Ballylee to his wife:

I, the poet William Yeats

With old millboards and

sea-green slates,

And smithy work from

the Gort forge,

Restored this tower for my wife George;

And may these characters

remain

When all is ruin once again.

LEFT: *Thoor Ballylee, home of the Yeates in Galway.*

The stone is still in place at Ballylee, the lines still legible; though until not so long ago the final line may have seemed prophetic. For after Yeats had died, the tower did fall to ruin again. But once more, through the efforts of local admirers and conservationists, Thoor Ballylee has been restored to much the same state as when the Yeatses lived there, and visitors can walk about its rooms.

During those long summer retreats to Galway with his wife and children, Yeats worked away on new plays and translations. He also produced some of his most enduring poetry – notably the volume of 36 poems, including *Sailing to Byzantium*, published in 1928. That he chose to call this volume after his poem, *The Tower*, is doubly significant when you are actually standing in Thoor Ballylee's shadow. For by now, that square Norman tower has become a symbol, almost a key, to the poet's gathering fury at the time's cruel advances. In this dark poem, the tower's great age and solidity hold out a glimmer of hope.

ABOVE: *Georgie; WB Yeats' wife.*

He returns again to the tower in *Meditations in Time of Civil War,* another dark and brooding poem, in which he contemplates the decay of once great houses like Coole Park and wonders whether Ireland would be any the better when they exist no more. But it is in the next section of the poem, *My House,* that he evokes the quiet beauties of Thoor Ballylee and stakes out for himself a place in history as its second founder – not as a man of arms this time, but by transforming the tower into a symbol of solitary thought and meditation that might outface time.

MEDITATIONS IN A TIME OF CIVIL WAR

II

My House

An ancient bridge, and a more ancient tower,

A farmhouse that is sheltered by its wall,

An acre of stony ground,

Where the symbolic rose can break in flower,

Old ragged elms, old thorns innumerable,

The sound of the rain or sound

Of every wind that blows;

The stilted water-hen

Crossing stream again

Scared by the splashing of a dozen cows;

A winding stair, a chamber arched with stone,

A grey stone fireplace with an open hearth,

A candle and written page.

Il Penseroso's Platonist toiled on

In some like chamber, shadowing forth

How the daemonic rage

Imagined everything.

Benighted travellers

From markets and from fairs

Have seen his midnight candle glimmering.

Two men have founded here. A man-at-arms

Gathered a score of horse and spent his days

In this tumultuous spot,

Where through long wars and sudden night alarms

His dwindling score and he seemed castaways

Forgetting and forgot;

And I, that after me

My bodily heirs may find,

To exalt a lonely mind,

Befitting emblems of adversity.

But what of the time when Yeats himself is dead and buried? How
would his austere idealism, so closely bound up in his mind with
the physical presence of the tower, fare then? The poet turns to
these matters in the fourth group of stanzas, uttering a terrible
curse should "my descendants lose the flower" before arriving at a
more confident resolution in the final lines.

MEDITATIONS

IV

My Descendants

Having inherited a vigorous mind

From my old fathers, I must nourish dreams

And leave a woman and a man behind

As vigorous of mind, and yet it seems

Life scarce can cast a fragrance on the wind,

Scarce spread a glory to the morning beams,

But the torn petals strew the garden plot;

And there's but common greenness after that.

And what if my descendants lose the flower

Through natural declension of the soul,

Through too much business with the passing hour,

Through too much play, or marriage with a fool?

May this laborious stair and this stark tower

Become a roofless ruin that the owl

May build in the cracked masonry and cry

Her desolation to the desolate sky.

The Primum Mobile that fashioned us

Has made the very owls in circles move;

And I, that count myself most prosperous,

Seeing that love and friendship are enough,

For an old neighbour's friendship chose the house

And decked and altered it for a girl's love,

And know whatever flourish and decline

These stones remain their monument and mine.

The note of defiance is still there; but by the time these lines were

published, much had changed in that corner of County Galway that

Yeats had made his spiritual home. Lady Gregory had been forced

through straitened circumstances to sell Coole Park to the Forestry

Department, though she was able to remain at the house for the

time being as a tenant. Most of the old trees in the Park had already

been cut down when Yeats recalled those happier days, when he and
other champions of Ireland's literary revival had been inspired at
Coole.

COOLE PARK, 1929

I meditate upon a swallow's flight,

Upon an aged woman and her house,

A sycamore and lime-tree lost in night

Although that western cloud is luminous,

Great works constructed there in nature's spite

For scholars and for poets after us,

Thoughts long knitted into a single thought,

A dance-like glory that those walls begot.

There Hyde before he had beaten into prose

That noble blade the Muses buckled on,

There one that ruffled in a manly pose

For all his timid heart, there that slow man,

That meditative man, John Synge, and those

Impetuous men, Shawe-Taylor and Hugh Lane,

Found pride established in humility,

A scene well set and excellent company.

They came like swallows and like swallows went,

And yet a woman's powerful character

Could keep a swallow to its first intent;

And half a dozen in formation there,

That seemed to whirl upon a compass-point,

Found certainty upon the dreaming air,

The intellectual sweetness of those lines

That cut through time or cross it withershins.

Here, traveller, scholar, poet, take your stand

When all those rooms and passages are gone,

When nettles wave upon a shapeless mound

And saplings root among the broken stone,

And dedicate – eyes bent upon the ground,

Back turned upon the brightness of the sun

And all the sensuality of the shade –

A moment's memory to that laurelled head.

Sadly, the final stanza's vision of a time "when nettles wave upon a shapeless mound" were all too prophetic.

There can be no doubting that W.B. Yeats mourned the passing of the Anglo-Irish gentry and their whole way of life. But it was not mere snobbery, nor delight in gracious living, that drew him to Lady Gregory's circle. As he acknowledges in the last poem, she kept him to composing his "half a dozen" lines each day. More than that, they shared a vision of a renascent Ireland. It was, of course, a very literary kind of renaissance, with its emphasis on rediscovering Irish myth and legend, reviving the dramatic arts in Ireland, raising the use of language – whether it be English, Gaelic or dialect – to new heights, and finally transmuting all of these elements into a sort of idealistic nationalism that was at once specifically Irish and yet inclusive.

It is as much the death or subversion of this idealism as the disappearance of "ancestral houses" like Coole that the ageing poet mourned. For all of this did indeed fall apart, and prove redundant, amidst the raw politics and civil wars of the 1920s.

At Coole Park, and later in his tower, Yeats seems to have absorbed his external surroundings until they became a part of himself. From images of external beauty he extracted a potent and enduring symbolism, which it seems has only grown more powerful with the passing of time. Could this have occurred were it not for the surroundings and the way of life he found in Galway? A passage which he wrote in 1909 may provide some clues:

> "Lady Gregory is planting trees; for a year they have taken much of her time. Her grandson will be fifty years old before they can be cut. We artists, do not we also plant trees and it is only after fifty years that we are of much value? Every day I notice some new analogy between the

long-established life of the well-born and the artist's life.

We come from the permanent things and create them,

and instead of old blood we have old emotions and we

carry in our heads always that form of society aristocracies

create now and again for some brief moment at Urbino or

Versailles. We too suffer at the hands of the mob…knowing

that our knowledge is invisible and that at the first breath

of ambition our dreams vanish. If we do not see daily

beautiful life at which we look as old men and women do

at young children, we become theorists – thinkers as it is

called, – or else give ourselves to strained emotions, to

some overflow of sentiment 'sighing after Jerusalem in the

regions of the grave'… How can we sing without our bush

of whins, our clump of heather, and does not Blake say it

takes a thousand years to create a flower?"

For Yeats, the poet's calling was an aristocratic one, born of "old

emotions" and containing the invisible forms of an ideal world.

ABOVE: *The Poets Cemetery, Killeeneen.*

Moreover, to give true expression to these emotions, to contain them within a disciplined austerity so that they speak more forcefully, the poet must daily see "the beautiful life." This is what Coole Park – and later Thoor Ballylee – gave up to Yeats. It is present even in those poems that do not overtly speak of Galway. Indeed, it may be said that rarely has a single place fed into the making of such great poetry as this hidden corner of Ireland.

And so it was with regret that I turned away from Yeats' tower, and headed back down country lanes, past old thatch cottages and stone walls, losing myself once more in Galway's iridescent landscape. Then by chance, at Killeeneen, I stumbled upon a poets' cemetery. Yeats chose to rest elsewhere; but these Galway poets have, each in their own way, also left their mark on Ireland's rich literary heritage. And while there were no Senators or Nobel Laureates buried in this simple graveyard, that did not matter. The very idea of a poets' cemetery in such an isolated spot... W.B would, I am sure, have approved.

IV

EPILOGUE

IN THE WINTER of 1938 the Yeatses went to the South of France, taking up residence in an hotel at Cap Martin. It was there that W.B. Yeats died of a heart attack on 28 January, 1939. He was 73 years old. His body was laid to rest, with Anglican prayers, in the Catholic cemetry at the nearby village of Roquebrune. Shortly before his death he had told his wife he wished to be reburied after a year in the churchyard of Drumcliff, County Sligo – the details of how the gravestone be made and its precise position being spelled out in his famous poem *Under Ben Bulben.*

LEFT: *Ben Bulben viewed from the dunes at Rosses Point.*

But before the year was out Europe was at war, and it was not until January 1948 that his remains were brought back aboard a fighting ship of the Irish Navy. The vessel docked at Galway, from whence the cortege proceeded to Sligo. The coffin, draped in the Irish tricolour, lay in state before Sligo's Town Hall, before being taken to the churchyard at Drumcliff and interred exactly as Yeats had specified.

Some forty years later a controversy arose over whether the body taken back from Roquebrune was indeed that of W.B. Yeats or a Captain Guillaume of the French Army. The questions then raised may never be completely settled.

I knew all this as I stood before the grave in Drumcliff Churchyard, and yet it did not seem to matter whether it was really Yeats down there or not. The legend of the man, the immortality of his verses, seemed to mock at any reasoned or "scientific" argument. If this was the final enigma, then this most enigmatic of poets would surely have smiled at it. That he stood high above the fray seemed to be confirmed by the words on his tombstone.

In spirit, he was there alright: of this is I was assured. For wherever he went in the world, Yeats was always returning to Ireland. For in Ireland he believed a "gift of vision" had been preserved as nowhere else. He had discovered this first as a young boy in the hills and valleys around Sligo, and it is fitting that here his spirit be laid to rest. It is where he always wanted to be.

ABOVE: *Yeats' grave in Drumcliff.*